OTAGO PENINSULA

PATH TO THE SEA

STEPHEN JAQUIERY

FOREWORD BY DAVID BELLAMY

Initial concept by Kathryn Hodgkinson and Richard Thomas

REED

REED PUBLISHING (NZ) LTD
TE KARUHI TĀ TĀPUI O REED (AOTEAROA)

Established in 1907, Reed is New Zealand's largest
book publisher, with over 600 titles in print.
www.reed.co.nz

Published by Reed Books, a division of Reed Publishing (NZ) Ltd,
39 Rawene Rd, Birkenhead, Auckland.
Associated companies, branches and representatives throughout the world.

Published by Reed Books

National Library of New Zealand Cataloguing-in-Publication Data
Jaquiery, Stephen, 1961-
Otago Peninsula : path to the sea / Stephen Jaquiery.
ISBN 978-0-7900-1127-1
1. Otago Peninsula (N.Z.)—Pictorial works. II. Title.
919.39200222—dc 22

ISBN-13 978 07900 1127 1
ISBN-10 0 7900 1127 1

Map illustration: Hayden Smith
Project editor: Gillian Tewsley
Cover design: Sarah Healey
Design: IslandBridge
Cover images: *Front:* Yellow-eyed penguins head out to sea at Otapahi
reserve. *Back:* Home to the Portobello Marine Studies Centre and
Aquarium, Quarantine Point extends into the Otago Harbour.

Printed in China

FOREWORD

Having had the privilege of visiting the Otago Peninsula and sharing breath, good counsel and an amazing diversity of natural food at a hangi on the Otakou marae, I am proud to add this wonderful book to my library.

This suberb rainbow of pictures allows you to hold whole land and seascapes in your hands, witness the march of the seasons and meet icons of the wilder world face to face. This book transports you on a nature-based tour of one of the world's most special and bounteous places — a tour of discovery, on which you will learn that people and wild things can live in harmony if only we all care enough.

Whether or not you decide to come and see the Peninsula for yourself, this book demands that you become one of the stewards of the natural world. Biodiversity is the most threatened of the world's resources. Always remember that every time a plant or animal goes to the wall of extinction it will be more difficult to stitch part of it back into sustainable working order. Time is running out: are you up to the challenge that this book lays before you?

Cherish every drop of water, become energy efficient, reduce, reuse and recycle and never ever throw plastic waste into the environment, for every piece threatens the survival of my three favourite icons of the Otago Peninsula: the royal albatross, the yellow-eyed penguin and Hector's dolphin.

Thank you for caring.

David Bellamy
The Mill House
Bedburn
June 2007

INTRODUCTION

Pohutukawa, the New Zealand Christmas tree, blossoms beside the road.

Recycling containers as letterboxes is a common practice in this part of the world.

Battered by the Pacific Ocean on one side, caressed by the harbour on the other, and with a high road along its spiny backbone, the Otago Peninsula is a wonderland of water, wildlife and stunning vistas. I have been a regular visitor to the Peninsula for the past 25 years, and some 50 dedicated excursions for this book have only made me more enthusiastic about the Peninsula's kaleidoscope of sights, constantly changing with the light, the tide and the seasons. I discover new highlights every time I visit. It can be dramatic in a storm, peaceful on a sunny day and, while often thronging with visitors, the Peninsula always reserves a few quiet spots for solitude.

With cameras tidily stowed, I usually set forth from the city, turned onto the Andersons Bay causeway, and headed along the sheltered harbour side. I look skyward and gauge the light. Does it offer good contrast or is it flat? Is the sky blue with delicious cottonball clouds, or grey and lifeless? Questions answered, I always relax, slow down and continue regardless.

The narrow, winding road demands respect as it follows the venerable harbour wall along the natural curves of the waterline. The wall was built from stone by prisoners doing 'hard labour' during the 1860s and 70s. Here I might smile at bumblebees drawn to flowering cabbage trees along the roadside in spring, or at honey bees in the fiery red pohutukawa flowers of summer. I relish the diversity of letterboxes and wonder about the characters who choose to have their mail delivered to a microwave oven or an old outboard motor. The artwork in the boxes made of natural materials such as paua shell or wood is something to behold.

I have never seen a boat moored at the jetty at Glenfalloch, but there is always a person or two enjoying a spot of fishing on a nice day. Most weekends, a wedding party can be seen gritting chattering teeth as a biting southerly takes the edge off the pleasure of being photographed outside.

I love the constantly changing water, glittering like diamonds one moment and smoking and crashing the next as a gale-force wind funnels down the harbour. The boatsheds are often charming, especially those that have been 'let go' a little: piles decaying and shell-encrusted, paint faded by sun and salt, rails covered in guano where shags perch, flat roofs mobbed by oystercatchers driven off their feeding beds by an incoming tide.

I am always ready to stop and admire a majestic royal spoonbill racking its oddly flattened beak through the water in search of food; or the slow, calculated and deliberate stalk of a white-faced heron before its lightning strike at a small, silver fish.

The ebbing tide is also the time to watch oystercatchers working away on an area of stones, turning them over one at a time with their strong beaks, and hammering the helpless limpets off for a tasty meal. Closer inspection has revealed black-backed gulls lifting shellfish high in the sky and dropping them onto rocks, over and over, until the sweet flesh is exposed. Finding a parking spot, I remain in my car, a long lens quietly protruding from the window so as not to disturb these daily displays.

Regular vessels such as log ships, oil tankers and container ships share the regularly dredged harbour channel with floating cruise ships that visit en masse during summer. Rowers in sleek boats prefer the still of early morning to train, while yacht racers wait for the breeze to strengthen later in the day.

Once, and only once, have I seen a small, vibrant green jewelled gecko, camouflaged beautifully in bushes at a secret spot. Every time I pass there now, I smile at the memory.

At Wellers Rock, a few fishing boats still scratch a living from the sea. This is also the site of a whaling station set up in 1831 to render whale blubber. Rocks still hold iron stanchions used to moor boats and tie up the whales during flensing.

If you have no interest in local arts and crafts, choose your travelling companion carefully, otherwise you may find yourself stopping an annoying number of times. Local artists fashion jewellery and paintings, as well as pottery, knives, brightly coloured clay hens (very popular), stone floormats and even the humble polished paua shells that are sold in shops and stalls dotted along the road from Macandrew Bay onward.

It is great to see the occasional New Zealand sealion on the beach near Harwood. Don't be deceived by their ponderous, lumbering gait on land; they can make a surprisingly fast lunge at careless spectators, so keep your distance.

Fur seals populate rocks on the northern end of Pilots Beach, access to which is very easy as you can drive to within a minute's walk of the beach. Crystal clear water allows a view of these sleek torpedoes. I have often photographed their endearing antics, water dripping off their long whiskers as they lounge back, their large black eyes quietly watchful and flippers crossed over their chest. It is hard to imagine that they were once slaughtered in tens of thousands for their pelts. People with a delicate disposition should not choose to eat their lunch at the seal colony; these mammals have a strictly fish diet, and the area exudes a distinctive pungent aroma.

At dusk, the little blue penguins return from their fishing expeditions and waddle up the beach before hopping over rocks to the sanctuary of their burrows.

The light of the setting sun bathes a fishing boat returning home from checking crayfish pots.

Wind-blown sand at Ryans Beach exposes a naturally polished paua shell.

The much-trumpeted royal albatross colony holds pride of place a short distance away on the headland. A chorus of squabbling seagulls are the first to greet visitors, landing on cars and depositing a white 'ticket' in greeting. From humble beginnings, when one man and a tent ensured the first successful albatross fledging at Taiaroa Head in 1938, a whole industry of protection and education has developed. The Royal Albatross Centre now attracts over 200,000 visitors every year. In a good year, there are up to 100 albatrosses in residence in this, the only mainland colony of albatross in the world. Predator protection work has made this a bird-friendly place.

If you are there when a stiff nor'easter wind is blowing, try wearing a white shirt while standing on the sea lookout below the carpark. You may soon be thrilled to find a majestic albatross swooping low to see if you are one of its own. Perched atop a sheer cliff face above the Pacific Ocean, the centre is also a great vantage point to observe spotted shags or be entertained by a nursery of red-billed gulls. They are constantly squawking, prodding and scrapping as they jostle for space. Young birds call for food while adults cruise updrafts.

The blue penguin is the smallest penguin, the average adult standing just 40 centimetres tall.

For the military-minded, gun emplacements litter the headland, a result of a perceived Russian threat in 1885. A tour will take you to the most impressive armament, the fully restored Armstrong disappearing gun, in a bunker beneath the albatross colony.

Backtracking, there is a short signposted detour to the Maori settlement of Otakou, which gave its name to the province of Otago. Here may be found a church, a wharenui (meeting house), and an urupa (cemetery) that contains the graves of several notable chiefs. There is also a memorial to the signing of the Treaty of Waitangi here on 13 June 1840, a local link with New Zealand's founding document.

The Otago Peninsula is one wall of a long dormant and deeply eroded volcano. The exposed ocean coast offers a marked contrast to the sheltered harbour side. I never tire of the two large estuaries at Papanui and Hoopers inlets, home to many waterbirds and seasonal visitors like the godwit flying in from the northern hemisphere. Sharp eyes are needed to spot the turquoise streak of a kingfisher's dive, while many other species of birds sit quietly and are quite used to admiring faces pressed against car windows.

The exposed coastal side of the Peninsula is often pounded by high seas.

The world's rarest penguin, the yellow-eyed penguin, takes pride of place on this coast. Intervention by conservationists is helping this species increase in numbers. In the crisp chill of pre-dawn, it is quite something to be standing on a hill watching these birds waddle off to sea to feed.

If you are feeling fit, there is a good walk to explore the basalt column rocks of the Pyramids near Victory Beach. Allans Beach is a short meander for the less fit, with a chance of encountering sealions on the beach or fur seals closer to the rocks at the northern end. Prepare for the weather: super-heated sand burns bare feet on a scorching day; and in a spectacular gale, this same sand stings exposed flesh and enters every cranny and crevice, including delicate camera equipment.

Back past Harbour Cone, a farmland track leads to the popular volcanic formations of the Chasm and Lovers Leap on the southern side of Hoopers Inlet at Sandymount. This is also where I ponder my mortality as I enviously watch hang-glider pilots launching on a northerly breeze and soaring with the birds.

Lovingly restored, Larnach Castle provides commanding views of the Otago Peninsula in all directions from its tower.

As the light fades, I head home for a late tea, down Highcliff Road past stone walls built by farming pioneers, and the Soldier's War Memorial standing proudly on a roadside hill.

I don't pretend this is a complete photographic record of the Otago Peninsula. Rather, it is a collection of images that excited the photographer in me.

I have enjoyed every one of my visits to the Peninsula. There have been highlights in encounters with the weather and the wildlife, and a profitable feed or two after discovering a good fishing spot or a new outcrop of mussels. My children have had the chance to get up close and personal with penguins and albatrosses, leave their footprints in the sand and have the salt air blown through their hair. I have met people from all places and backgrounds who share my enthusiasm for this beguiling place.

My photographs, I hope, convey something of the unique character and beauty of this special corner of New Zealand. Perhaps, also, those well acquainted with the area will find in these images lasting reminders of spectacular scenes from their own experiences on the Otago Peninsula.

Stephen Jaquiery
Dunedin, 2007

Taiaroa Head lighthouse, built in 1864–65, shares the tip of the Peninsula with an array of bird life.

Larnach Castle. Despite many visits, I have still not encountered the rumoured resident ghost.

Taiaroa
Head

Harington Pt

Te Rauone Beach

Penguin
Beach

Pipikaretu
Beach

Ryans Beach

Otakou

Harwood

Portobello Bay

Portobello

Harbour Cone

Quarantine Is

Larnach Castle

Broad Bay

MONARCH

Company Bay

Highcliff Rd

Castlewood Rd

Macandrew Bay

Glenfalloch

Highcliff
War memorial

Highcliff Rd

Centre

Portobello Rd

Tomahawk Lagoon

Burns Pt

Vauxhall

Highcliff Rd

Andersons Bay
Inlet

St Clair Beach

Lawyers
Head

amids

Victory Beach

Titikoraki

Mt Charles

Papanui Beach

Otewhata

Cape Saunders

Matakitaki Pt

Papanui Inlet

i Flat

Lime kilns

Hoopers Inlet

Allans Beach

Sandymount

Sandymount Rd

The Chasm

Lovers Leap

Sandfly Bay

Harakeke Pt

Gull Rocks

Seal Pt

Boulder Beach

Highcliff

Maori Head

Smaills Beach

hawk Beach

Nature colours sky and harbour
to create special effects for early
risers in midwinter.

The massive, creamy flower heads of the palm-like cabbage tree (ti kouka) emerge in spring and last well into summer.

Left

Bus shelters illustrating the character of their surrounds are a feature of the Peninsula. This one, depicting the White House, stands on a historic site where, in times past, visitors from Dunedin would step ashore from a ferry on their journey to Larnach Castle.

Opposite

Spring marks the start of the busy wedding season for the Glenfalloch Woodland Gardens. Owned by the Otago Peninsula Trust since 1967, the original kauri homestead of George Gray Russell is now used regularly for functions.

His lines dangling in the water, a fisherman dozes off on the Glenfalloch wharf. Colour is the very essence of the Peninsula's charm yet, at times, its absence allows us to appreciate the the simple beauty of line and form.

A pool of light on Blanket Bay gives hope that a misty afternoon may yet clear.

Left

Home to over 1100 residents, Macandrew Bay is a 10-kilometre harbourside drive from the centre of Dunedin. Named after James Macandrew, a notable figure in the early days of Dunedin, the Bay is both a commuter town and a popular harbourside retreat.

Right

Harbour Cone has dominated the Peninsula skyline for 10 million years.

Opposite

A Broad Bay boatshed doubles as a colourful billboard for a local potter.

Right

Free parking is always popular and these red-billed gulls in Latham Bay, Portobello, are happy to provide a free paint job for the privilege.

Boats can be philosophers too. This yacht, lying lazily at
its mooring, spends whole days simply reflecting ...

Not her usual crew, but enthusiastic replacements;
shags take over an abandoned craft in Edwards Bay.

Exported throughout the world, these gaily coloured ceramic Happy Hens have their origins at Portobello. The Peninsula is a haven for artists and craft enthusiasts, with studios and stalls adding human interest to its historic and scenic attractions.

Past and present merge as a 1927 Essex trundles past the Portobello pub during a motorcycle rally.

Erected to help motorists see round a tight corner on the gravel road to the Portobello Marine Studies Centre and Aquarium, this mirror also lets pedestrians check their appearance.

If you want to keep up with the Joneses of the sheep
world, a stylish enamelled water trough is a must.

Sharp eyes are required to spot
this jewelled gecko soaking up
the sun in coprosma bushes.

The harbour road, protected from water erosion by a
stacked stone wall, is popular with fitness enthusiasts.

Fairy Prion, named after a dainty, fairy-like petrel, rests quietly at anchor in Portobello Bay. Built as a lifeboat in the United Kingdom in 1930, this clinker-style boat has had a cabin added and now serves as a private pleasure craft.

Above

A variable oystercatcher rolls over a stone while searching for molluscs, which it will then prise out of the shell with its powerful beak.

Right

Extensive flats, uncovered at low tide near Harwood, make a tranquil exercise ground for horse and human alike.

Black-backed gulls rest on the incoming tide as
it surrounds this boatshed in Portobello Bay.

Nature's clothesline: seaweed snagged on a mooring line
is washed then dried with the ebb and flow of the tide.

A dinghy at anchor in Portobello Bay. The many indentations and anchorages on the harbour side of the Peninsula provide a paradise for all who enjoy the simple pleasure of 'mucking about in boats'.

Where whales were once winched ashore at Otakou, a small fishing industry still exists. Today, these activities are watched over by the ubiquitous sheep.

An intricately carved gateway marks the entrance to the Otakou marae, a site of ancient Maori occupation. Notable chiefs of the nineteenth century now rest in the marae cemetery.

Left

An outboard motor is recycled as a letterbox.

Right

The tide ebbs below an Otakou boatshed.

Aramoana sand-flats are exposed by a falling tide as the first rays of sun fall on Dunedin city at the head of the harbour.

45

Early risers on *The World* — the first ocean-going residential ship, seen here on her inaugural visit to Dunedin — are treated to a spectacular sunrise.

Harington Point near Taiaroa Head is a long way from the grocer, but not far from the harbourside larder. Fishing is a popular pastime with residents and holiday makers here. Boatsheds are colourful and conspicuous along the water's edge.

The tourist vessel *Monarch* cuts a wave during a daily wildlife observation cruise.

Above

A sealion lumbers up Te Rauone Beach near the settlement at Harington Point. Adult male sealions can weigh at least 450 kilograms and measure over three metres in length.

Right

In spite of being nearly wiped out by early hunters, fur seals are now thriving around the Otago Peninsula, happily sharing their habitat with other wildlife, including the two-legged creatures who were once their enemy.

Red-billed gulls breed in a noisy colony on sheer cliffs at Taiaroa Head.

A white-faced heron shows off its plumage.

Taiaroa Head, at the tip of the Peninsula,
is the only mainland colony of albatross
in the world.

Only a few days old, this northern royal albatross chick at Taiaroa Head
will not be ready to leave the colony for another eight and a half months.

Left

Albatross have an average life-span of thirty-five years.

Above

Locals ignore the threat of an approaching storm to wave farewell
to the cruise ship *Sapphire Princess* on its way out of the harbour.

Right

The Mole, a man-made breakwater, protects the Otago Harbour
entrance on the northern side, while Taiaroa Head shelters the
southern side. The rugged and exposed Pacific coast of the
Peninsula offers dramatic scenery and a diverse array of wildlife.

Natural forces shape the coast and the vegetation at remote Ryans Beach.

A shallow cave frames Quoin Cliff at the northen end of
Ryans Beach — a vista begging to be used as a film set.

Sand slowly envelops the shipwreck of the *Hananui II* on Ryans Beach.
The fishing boat ran aground in 1943 after being caught in thick fog.

The Antarctic to the south and the vast reach of the encircling Pacific ensure constantly varying weather on the Peninsula. Cirrus clouds like these are a sign that strong winds are on the way.

Clinging to the rocks regardless of incessant surf and ferocious storms,
bull kelp swirls in the ocean off Te Whakarekaiwi headland.

The New Zealand sealion should become a more common sight on the
Peninsula with the recent establishment of a breeding colony on the coast.

Left and above

A southern right whale, displaying its narrow tail flukes, passes Victory Beach in Wickliffe Bay. This species is now increasing in numbers after being hunted nearly to extinction in the early 1800s.

Above

Westerly winds whip the tops off waves rolling into Victory Beach, where the distinctive Pyramids rock formation stands.

Left

Popular with both wildlife and humans alike, the unspoilt Allans Beach is isolated to the south by the sea entrance to Hoopers Inlet, but is quite accessible from its northern end via a short track from Allans Beach road.

Back from fishing at sea, a New Zealand sealion blends
into the beach, its wet hide coated with sand.

Papanui Beach at the approach of dawn.

The few remaining leaves on this elderly cabbage tree
above Wickliffe Bay battle a gale-force southwest wind.

Travelling by air with a very flexible itinerary, a
feather rests in the gentle grasp of a seedhead.

Left

Careys Bay fishing boat *Sanspeur* approaches a craypot buoy set at Cape Saunders.

Right

A few days later, Matakitaki Point where the Cape Saunders lighthouse sits is given a salty wash by a southerly swell.

Above

As the wind batters the exposed Cape Saunders headland,
newborn lambs find relative comfort under snow tussocks.
Is that a look of stoicism or resignation on their faces?

Right

Golden-coloured tussocks bend their heads as strong southerlies
push storm clouds towards the steep-sided stack of Wharekakahu.

A contrast to the fierce Peninsula storms is the peaceful tranquillity of early morning on Hoopers Inlet.

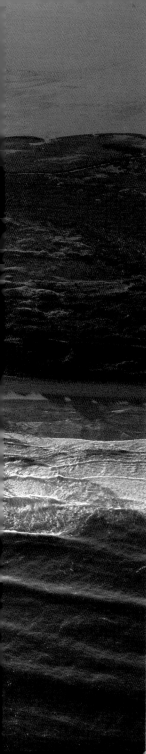

Left

Looking down on Hoopers Inlet, it is easy to see how a build-up of sand occasionally closes the entrance.

Right

Perched on a rusty boatshed, a kingfisher watches for unsuspecting prey emerging from the sand at low tide.

The distinctive form of Pukemata (Harbour Cone) rises above Hoopers Inlet.

Overleaf

An aerial view dominated by Harbour Cone reveals the undulating nature of the Peninsula. The estuaries of Hoopers and Papanui inlets are on the right.

A royal spoonbill shakes water off its feathers.

An adult pied stilt keeps protectively close to its chick.

Left

This derelict house overlooking Hoopers Inlet has certainly seen better days, but evidence inside suggests it is now used as an occasional shelter for livestock.

Above

A fantail rests on a fence wire that has been well rusted by the salt-laden air.

Moove over: a warning sign on Castlewood Road.

A common gecko, seen here blending into the colours
of the rock, is an unusual sight on the Peninsula.

One way to enjoy the views of the Peninsula is
to take on the challenge of a brisk uphill walk.

Dairy heifers hoof it down Centre Road.

Built in 1871, Larnach Castle fell into disrepair in later years before being lovingly restored by the Barker family. The castle now plays host to over 100,000 visitors every year.

Deep snow does not often blanket the Peninsula; and
even this fall at Larnach Castle will thaw by lunchtime.

A stargazer is treated to a spectacular display from Comet McNaught in 2007.
The lights of Port Chalmers are at right and Larnach Castle to the left.

Wind-driven snow plasters the
weather-side of macrocarpa trees
on Camp Road and a fencepost
on Highcliff Road.

Hang-gliders soar like birds on the uplifting airflow when northerly winds blow towards Sandymount from Hoopers Inlet.

Above

A native fly (*Protohystricia alcis*) soaks up the sun on a broadleaf post above Lovers Leap. As a parasite of the pasture-destroying porina moth's caterpillar, this is one of New Zealand's most beneficial insects.

Right

Years of prevailing winds have shaped these macrocarpa to form an arch over Sandymount Road.

Ironically, as they walk through the macrocarpa avenue, this wedding couple is heading in the direction of a spectacular natural feature — Lovers Leap!

Testimony to the stonemason's skill, historic lime kilns still stand near Sandymount.
The kilns, built in the 1860s, were used to burn limestone for cement.

The sun rises over Gull Rocks off Sandfly Bay.

Marram grass dances in the wind at Sandfly Bay on a stormy day. Backed by deep sand dunes, Sandfly Bay is attractive to seals and yellow-eyed penguins, as well as people.

The rising sun emerges above the horizon,
sharpening the outline of Matakitaki Point.

Keen yellow-eyed penguin observers gather at a hillside
vantage point to watch the pre-dawn march to the sea.

Otago Peninsula is home to the largest mainland colony of
yellow-eyed penguins in the world. The penguin gains its
name from its yellow irises and distinctive yellow headband.

Pounding hooves are drowned
out by pounding surf as trotters
are exercised on Smaills Beach.

Scenes over looking Macandrew Bay taken from
a popular photographic spot on Highcliff Road,
in winter (left) and in spring (above).

Stone walls, built using the stones cleared from new paddocks, still crisscross the Peninsula, bearing testimony to the skills, industry and heritage of the first European settlers.

Superseded by milk tankers, these milk cans
now support a letterbox on Highcliff Road.

In a final performance for the day, the last rays of
the sun transfigure a fence on Highcliff Road.

Unveiled in 1923, this memorial to fallen soldiers is set dramatically on a massive rock that offers views of the harbour, city and coastline.

Neither floodlighting nor any other illumination can compare
in dramatic effect with a full moon, well positioned.

Viewed from Highcliff Road,
Dunedin city lights sparkle
at dusk.

127

ABOUT THE AUTHORS

Described recently by a senior New Zealand columnist as 'a living treasure', **Stephen Jaquiery** has never been more successful than during the period when he was taking photographs for this book. He was named Qantas Senior Photographer of the Year, and also staged a *City Birds* exhibition at the Otago Museum that was viewed by a record 80,000 people. Now a household name in Otago, Stephen has worked as a photographer for the *Otago Daily Times* for 27 years. He has spent many hundreds of hours on the Otago Peninsula, photographing its people, wildlife and scenery, walking its tracks, enjoying the extensive beaches and hauling up blue cod from his boat.

Entranced by the Otago Peninsula, Australian-born **Kathryn Hodgkinson** co-produced a half-hour documentary film about the area as part of her postgraduate diploma in natural history filmmaking and communication at the University of Otago in 2004. Kathryn's passion for wildlife and nature photography, combined with her genuine appreciation of the Peninsula, were the inspiration for this book, which captures the true essence of the Otago Peninsula and its many fascinating creatures.

In his television career **Richard Thomas** has worked in major cities in the UK, Australia (as director of television for the Australian Broadcasting Corporation) and New Zealand, most recently at Natural History New Zealand in Dunedin. Each day as he walked to work there, he looked out to the Peninsula — the striking natural history paradise a mere five minutes' drive from the city. Wanting to share it with the world, he sought in vain for a book – so he decided to change that . . .